SPOTLIGHT ON GEORGIA

GEORGIA DURING WORLD WAR II

SAM CROMPTON

PowerKiDS press

NEW YORK

Published in 2018 by The Rosen Publishing Group, Inc.
29 East 21st Street, New York, NY 10010

Editor: Elizabeth Krajnik
Book Design: Michael Flynn
Interior Layout: Reann Nye

Photo Credits: Cover, p. 11 Courtesy of the Georgia Historical Society; p. 5 https://commons.wikimedia.org/wiki/File:Hells_Angels,_Flying_Tigers_1942.jpg; p. 6 https://commons.wikimedia.org/wiki/File:FDR_1944_Color_Portrait.tif; p. 7 Bettmann/Getty Images; p. 8 https://commons.wikimedia.org/wiki/File:The_USS_Arizona_(BB-39)_burning_after_the_Japanese_attack_on_Pearl_Harbor_-_NARA_195617_-_Edit.jpg; p. 9 https://commons.wikimedia.org/wiki/File:USS_Arizona_Memorial_(aerial_view).jpg; pp. 12, 16, 27 Courtesy of the Library of Congress; p. 13 https://en.wikipedia.org/wiki/File:Jaj074.jpg; p. 15 Courtesy of Kennesaw State University Archives; p. 15 (background) Reinhold Leitner/Shutterstock.com; p. 17 Hulton Deutsch/Corbis Historical/Getty Images; p. 18 https://commons.wikimedia.org/wiki/File:BT-13_Valiant.jpg; p. 19 https://commons.wikimedia.org/wiki/File:Bainbridge_Army_Airfield_-_Oblique_Airphoto.jpg; p. 21 Ted Russell/The LIFE Images Collection/Getty Images; p. 23 https://en.wikipedia.org/wiki/Carl_Vinson#/media/File:Carl_Vinson_(D%E2%80%93GA).jpg; p. 25 Myron Davis/The LIFE Picture Collection/Getty Images; p. 26 Courtesy of the Rome Area History Museum; p. 28 Historical/Corbis Historical/Getty Images; p. 29 Courtesy of Georgia State University Library Archives.

Cataloging-in-Publication Data

Names: Crompton, Sam.
Title: Georgia during World War II / Sam Crompton.
Description: New York : PowerKids Press, 2018. | Series: Spotlight on Georgia | Includes index.
Identifiers: ISBN 9781508159964 (pbk.) | ISBN 9781508159995 (library bound) | ISBN 9781508159971 (6 pack)
Subjects: LCSH: Georgia--History--Juvenile literature. | Georgia--Juvenile literature.
Classification: LCC F286.3 C76 2018 | DDC 975.8--dc23

Manufactured in the United States of America

CPSIA Compliance Information: Batch #BS17PK For further information contact Rosen Publishing, New York, New York at 1-800-237-9932.

CONTENTS

CHAPTER ONE

THE CAUSES OF WAR

World War II lasted from 1939 to 1945. In Europe, the war began when German **dictator** Adolf Hitler's army **invaded** Poland on September 1, 1939. France and Great Britain, Poland's **allies**, declared war against Germany on September 3, 1939.

Japan saw the war in Europe as an opportunity to quickly grow its empire in Southeast Asia by seizing European colonies, so it allied itself with Germany. However, the main obstacle to this goal would be the United States. Japan's attempt to remove that obstacle by attacking Pearl Harbor in Hawaii would lead to the United States entering the war in 1941.

Although the United States didn't **declare** its involvement in the war until then, many people contributed to the war effort before this. The people of Georgia did their part by sending trained soldiers and making airplanes and ships.

The Flying Tigers were a group of American volunteer pilots who flew as part of the Chinese Air Force. They defended China from Japanese attack. Their aircraft are some of the most recognizable planes from World War II. Robert Lee Scott Jr. was a fighter pilot from Macon, Georgia, who flew alongside the Flying Tigers.

CHAPTER TWO

AIDING ALLIES TO KEEP AMERICA SAFE

From the beginning, the war in Europe took a great **toll** on many of America's allies. By December 1940, Great Britain was almost **bankrupt**. On March 11, 1941, less than a year before the United States entered World War II, the House of Representatives voted to approve the Lend-Lease Act. President Franklin D. Roosevelt, also known as FDR, signed the bill into law. This act allowed the president to give aid to U.S. allies in the form of military equipment and other items to keep America safe from foreign attack.

FRANKLIN D. ROOSEVELT

Colonel Charles Lindbergh was one of many isolationists who opposed the Lend-Lease Act. He felt very strongly about keeping the United States out of the war.

Many people, called internationalists, agreed with FDR's decision to sign this bill into law. However, people known as isolationists were upset with him. They thought this was a step toward entering the war. Soon, Georgia would begin producing more equipment to contribute to the war effort.

CHAPTER THREE

"A DATE WHICH WILL LIVE IN INFAMY"

Although the United States hadn't entered the war yet, that didn't mean the country wasn't a target. Japan didn't want the United States to interfere with its expansion plans, which included Australia and Hawaii. The Japanese decided to try a swift and overwhelming attack to eliminate U.S. ships.

USS *ARIZONA*
DECEMBER 7, 1941

The wreckage of the USS *Arizona* lies just beneath the surface of the water in Pearl Harbor. Five men from Georgia died on the *Arizona*. A memorial to honor all those who lost their lives on the battleship was dedicated on May 30, 1962.

Early on the morning of Sunday, December 7, 1941, the U.S. naval base at Pearl Harbor, Hawaii, was attacked by Japanese airplanes. Eight battleships were harbored at the time, and a number of them were sunk. Nearly 200 aircraft were also destroyed in the attacks. More than 2,300 military members and 68 non-military people died that day. President Franklin D. Roosevelt called it "a date which will live in **infamy**." The U.S. Congress declared war against Japan on December 8.

CHAPTER FOUR

GEORGIA BUILDS LIBERTY SHIPS

Prior to the Lend-Lease Act in 1941, the government created the United States Maritime Commission (MARCOM). This federal agency built large cargo ships that were used to send supplies to U.S. allies. These ships were known as Liberty ships. They were designed to carry heavy loads and could be built quickly and inexpensively. The first Liberty ship was launched in September 1941.

The MARCOM established 18 shipyards on the East and West Coasts to build Liberty ships. Two of these shipyards were in Brunswick and Savannah, Georgia. The Savannah shipyard launched its first Liberty ship, the SS *James Oglethorpe*, in November 1942. In 1943, the Savannah shipyard employed 15,000 people, 3,500 of whom were women, from the greater Savannah area and from around the country. Throughout the war, the Savannah shipyard produced 88 Liberty ships.

Many Liberty ships were named after well-known or influential people from United States history. The SS *Crawford Long* was named after a surgeon and **pharmacist** from Georgia.

About a year after production began at the Savannah shipyard, Liberty ship production began in Brunswick. The shipyard **christened** its first Liberty ship, the SS *James M. Wayne*, in February 1943. At the shipyard's peak of production, it employed around 16,000 people, including 1,000 women. Most workers came from rural farming backgrounds and many were from Georgia. However, people from small towns throughout the South were also employed there. By the end of the war, Brunswick shipyard produced 85 Liberty ships.

Because these shipyards employed so many people, the economies of these two cities were lifted from their post-Great Depression slump. Many of the Savannah shipyard's employees invested money from their paychecks in bonds, which helped support the war. Some historians credit the Liberty ships with helping to save America's allies and the world.

JOSEPH M. TERRELL

The SS *Joseph M. Terrell*, which was constructed at the Brunswick shipyard, was named after the United States senator and 57th governor of Georgia.

CHAPTER FIVE

BELL BOMBER AND THE B-29S

The United States supplied its allies with food and military equipment, including fighter planes. The attack on Pearl Harbor made the United States government wary of producing war materials on the coasts, where an attack would be easier. In 1942, Bell Aircraft Corporation opened a plant in Marietta, Georgia. This was near Atlanta, which had railroad depots and an airport. The Marietta plant was also near Rickenbacker Field airstrip, where planes could land and take off. Starting in 1943 this plant began building the B-29 Superfortress, which was the country's largest bomber at the time.

The plant, known as Bell Bomber, helped the local economy. At its peak in February 1945, Bell Bomber employed 28,158 people. About 37 percent of these workers were women. Many employees came from north Georgia, and almost all employees were from the South. By the end of the war, employees at Bell Bomber had constructed 668 B-29s.

KK Now when you went to Bell, what kinds of job openings were there and what led you to the job that you took?

ES I can tell you what I did. It was something like the finishing department where they sent all parts that went into the airplane, regardless of how small they were, through some kind of treatment process. We would clean those parts, and they would put it in a machine and then some kind of solution and what-have-you. I don't know whether it was strengthening or just to be sure it was clean or what. And then sometimes, after they had got a part of the plane completed, we'd go inside of that plane and clean it all in the inside. Those long parts to the plane, sometimes we'd have to take something like steel wool and rub them; and then they would put them through this process I'm telling you about. And the little, bitty pieces like that, we had in the buckets, we'd drop them in. They'd put them through this process.

KK Did you work Monday through Friday?

ES Yes, yes, I did.

KK From like nine to five?

ES No, I went on the evening shift.

KK Because your husband -- that's right, your husband was working days.

ES Yes. We would go in around 11:00 or 11:45 and work until -- now my older children had started to school. And see, I'd get here early enough to see that all was well with them and that their clothes and everything were on properly and so forth, and they could get to school without being late.

KK Uh-huh. So you went to work at what time, then?

ES I think it was around 12:00, 12:45.

KK Was that noon or at midnight?

ES At night -- midnight.

In 1992, Kathryn Kelley (KK) interviewed Emestine Slade (ES). Slade was one of the many women who worked at Bell Bomber during World War II. She made $34 a week. Slade, an African American, had been paid much less at her previous jobs.

CHAPTER SIX

PREPARING TO FIGHT

Georgia had many military installations, or bases where military members live, work, and train. There were installations in almost every major city in Georgia. Fort Benning in Columbus is the largest infantry training school in the world. It was established as Camp Benning in 1918 and named after Henry L. Benning, a brigadier general during the Civil War.

In 1940, the Second Armored Division was formed at Fort Benning. Fort Benning was also home to the 555th Parachute Infantry Battalion, or the Triple Nickles. This group of African American troops trained at Fort Benning but never went overseas. The Fourth Infantry Division went through basic training at Fort Benning before it was sent to fight in Germany.

Robins Air Force Base, located just outside Macon, Georgia, opened in 1942 and is still in use today. More than 23,000 people worked there during the war years, repairing different types of aircraft.

Soldiers trained to jump from airplanes with parachutes at Fort Benning.

Different types of military installments operated in Georgia during World War II. In Chamblee, U.S. Naval Air Station (NAS) Atlanta trained naval and Marine Corps pilots. People from throughout the Southeast traveled to the base for training. By training these pilots, the NAS contributed to the United States' success in winning the war.

VULTEE BT-13

Bainbridge Air Base was built in Bainbridge, Georgia, in 1942. The airfield was used as a training facility. The first training group flew with 75 Vultee BT-13s.

At Camp Gordon—now Fort Gordon, near Augusta, Georgia—men trained to fight in and support the U.S. Army. Camp Gordon was known as one of the army's most important training facilities during World War II. Three divisions of the army were based at Camp Gordon. These included the Fourth Infantry, the 26th Infantry, and the 10th Armored. Each division was sent to fight in the war in Europe. The United States also held prisoners of war at the camp from 1943 to 1945.

CHAPTER SEVEN

RUSSELL'S CONTRIBUTIONS TO THE WAR

Richard B. Russell Jr. was an important figure in Georgia's period of economic growth before, during, and after World War II. He served as a state legislator, governor of Georgia, and U.S. senator.

Russell's most important work happened while he was a U.S. senator from 1933 until his death in 1971. He became heavily invested in military affairs during World War II. He traveled to many countries with fellow senators to talk about America's involvement in the war. Russell approved of international military bases to make sure that America would be safe during foreign wars.

Despite Russell's positive contributions to the war effort, he remained an isolationist. He also fought to keep the South segregated and opposed civil rights legislation.

Russell worked hard to support Georgia's economy. He secured or kept 15 military installations and 25 research facilities in the state. He also worked to get more federal funding for **infrastructure**.

CHAPTER EIGHT

"TWO-OCEAN NAVY"

Like Russell, Carl Vinson of Georgia made great strides for the United States' involvement in the war. Vinson served in the House of Representatives from 1914 to 1965. He took a seat on the Naval Affairs Committee in 1917 and used this position to work toward a greater U.S. military presence on the water and in the air.

Before America's entry into World War II, Vinson played an important role in two military bills. These bills increased the United States' number of aircraft, pilots, and air bases and allowed for quicker naval shipbuilding. His involvement in boosting the country's national defense—especially the navy—earned him two nicknames: "the Admiral" and "the father of the two-ocean navy." Vinson made it possible for America's navy to fight in both the Pacific and the Atlantic areas of the war.

During his time in the House of Representatives, Vinson represented a district that was surrounded by land. Despite this, Vinson's support for the U.S. Navy helped the Allies win the war.

CHAPTER NINE

BOOSTING GEORGIA'S ECONOMY

Georgia's role as a center of industry during World War II brought it out of the ashes and dust left behind from the Great Depression. Before the war began, many politicians saw Georgia as an economic burden on the country. Families in Georgia earned less money than families in many other states. However, America and its allies' need for military supplies launched Georgia from poverty into a booming economy.

The shipyards at Savannah and Brunswick and the Bell Bomber plant in Marietta brought more people into the state. The workers were paid higher wages than Georgia had seen in over 50 years.

After the United States' entry into the war, military bases drew employees and soldiers alike to Georgia. The development of these bases increased the population of the surrounding cities. This economic growth continued well into the 1950s.

Ellis Arnall was Georgia's governor from 1943 to 1947. During his term, Arnall paid off Georgia's debt and fought hard to help the state's economy recover from the Great Depression.

CHAPTER TEN

TEXTILES FOR TROOPS

Georgia was an important area of **textile** production for the war effort. During the early 20th century, there were many problems in this industry, such as labor strikes. After the war broke out, many positive changes took place. Textile factories hired many new workers to meet the demand for wartime supplies.

The American Chatillon Corporation in Rome, Georgia, produced a type of man-made silk called rayon for parachutes. This fiber was much less expensive than silk, which kept manufacturing costs low for textile companies.

AMERICAN CHATILLON CORPORATION
ROME, GEORGIA

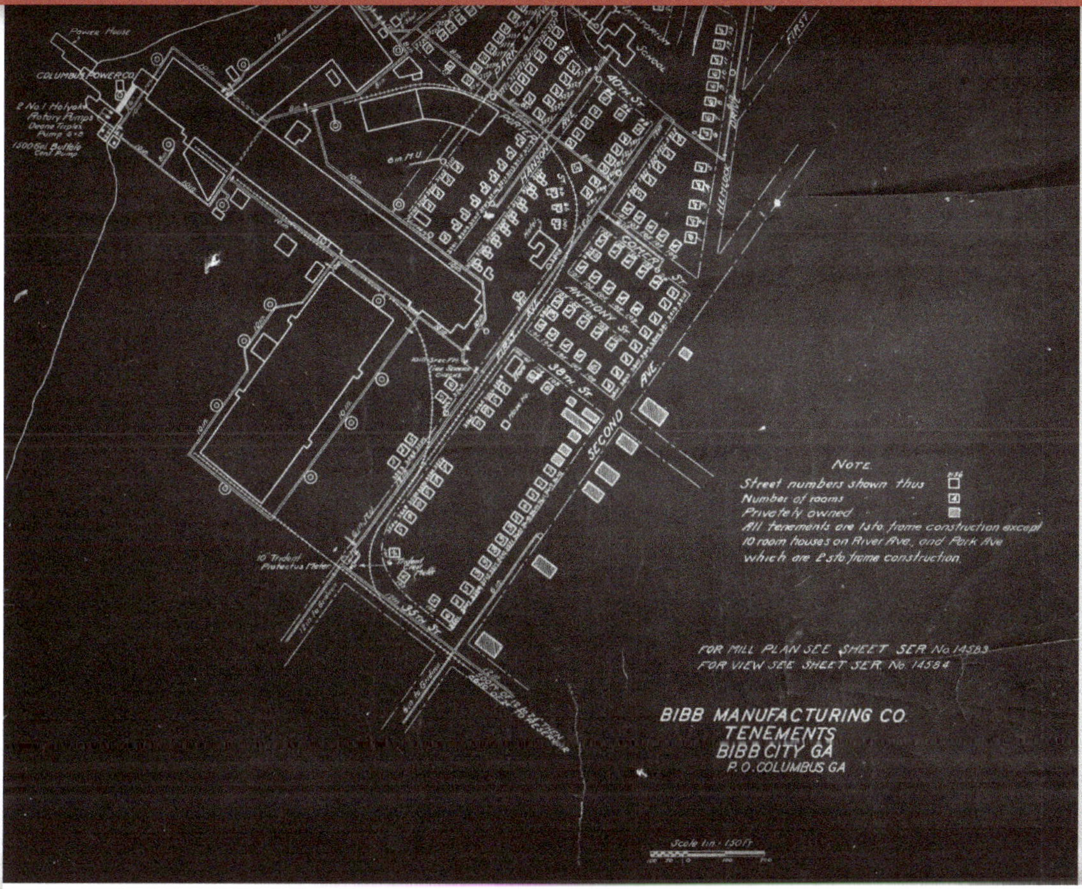

The Bibb Manufacturing Company created the company town of Bibb City near Columbus, Georgia, around a textile mill. The town had its own school, auditorium, church, and swimming pool.

The Bibb Manufacturing Company was the largest war-industry textile producer in the United States and one of Georgia's largest employers. The company had several different mills throughout the state. The Columbus mill was located on the Chattahoochee River near Columbus, Georgia. It produced **camouflage**, nets, life rafts, gas masks, and uniforms for soldiers.

CHAPTER ELEVEN

WOMEN'S ROLES IN THE WAR

Women played an especially important part in Georgia's economy during World War II. When the United States entered the war in 1941, women became responsible for providing for their families in the absence of men who joined the military. Some women chose to join the Women's Army Auxiliary Corps, which allowed women to serve in the military without being nurses.

The many new factories in Georgia needed workers, and women took jobs at them to make money and contribute to the war effort. At the Brunswick shipyard, women quickly moved up the ranks. By mid-September 1942, nine of the women who were originally hired to be secretaries were trained as **welders**. These women inspired others to work hard in what were usually considered men's positions. By February 1943, 12 women had passed an American Bureau of Ships test allowing them to work as skilled welders.

Rosie the Riveter (left) represented the women who contributed to the war effort by working in factories. These women changed many people's outlooks on traditional women's roles during the mid-20th century.

CHAPTER TWELVE

THE WAR'S END

Less than one month before the war's end, President Franklin D. Roosevelt paid his last visit to one of his favorite places—Warm Springs, Georgia. FDR died April 12, 1945, in Warm Springs as he posed for a portrait. Many people were saddened by his death, including British Prime Minister Winston Churchill.

May 8, 1945, marked the official end of the war in Europe and September 2, 1945, marked the end of the war in the Pacific. More than 400,000 Americans died because of the war and over 60 million died worldwide. Over 5,000 soldiers from Georgia lost their lives.

Georgia's economy was stronger during World War II than it had been since before the Civil War. Georgia's economy would continue to grow and become more modern in the years following the war.

GLOSSARY

ally (AA-ly) A person or country associated with another for a common purpose, or to join for a common purpose.

bankrupt (BANK-ruhpt) To be in a state of financial ruin.

camouflage (KAA-muh-flaj) The green and brown clothing that soldiers wear to make them harder to see.

christen (KRIH-suhn) To officially give a ship a name in a ceremony.

declare (dih-KLAYR) To officially announce.

dictator (DIK-tay-tuhr) A person who takes power and has total control over others.

infamy (IN-fuh-mee) An evil or terrible act, or an evil reputation.

infrastructure (IN-fruh-struk-chur) The system of public works of a country, state, or region.

invade (in-VAYD) To enter an area to take control of it by military force.

pharmacist (FAR-muh-sist) A person whose job is to prepare and sell the drugs and medicines that a doctor prescribes for patients.

textile (TEK-styl) A kind of cloth that is woven or knit.

toll (TOHL) The cost in life or health.

welder (WEL-duhr) A person whose work is joining pieces of metal together by heating the edges until they begin to melt and then pressing them together.

INDEX

PRIMARY SOURCE LIST

Page 15
Interview with Emestine J. Slade. Conducted by Kathryn A. Kelley for the Cobb County Oral History Senes, No. 28. April 28, 1992 and May 19, 1992. Courtesy of Kennesaw State University Archives.

Page 16
Student paratrooper about to land at Fort Benning, Georgia. Negative. Created in April 1942. Now kept at the Library of Congress Prints and Photographs Division, Washington, D.C.

Page 27
Bibb Manufacturing Company city plan for Bibb City. Blueprint. Now kept at the Library of Congress Prints and Photographs Division, Washington, D.C.

WEBSITES

Due to the changing nature of Internet links, PowerKids Press has developed an online list of websites related to the subject of this book. This site is updated regularly. Please use this link to access the list: www.powerkidslinks.com/sog/wwii